PAIGE BUECKERS

CHARLIE BEATTIE

WWW.APEXEDITIONS.COM

Copyright © 2026 by Apex Editions, Mendota Heights, MN 55120. All rights reserved. No part of this book may be reproduced or utilized in any form or by any means without written permission from the publisher.

Apex is distributed by North Star Editions:
sales@northstareditions.com | 888-417-0195

Produced for Apex by Red Line Editorial.

Photographs ©: Abbie Parr/AP Images, cover, 1; Dan Heary/Eclipse Sportswire/Cal Sport Media/AP Images, 4–5; Frank Franklin II/AP Images, 6–7; Shutterstock Images, 8–9, 12–13; Hannah Foslien/Getty Images Sport/Getty Images, 10–11; Marcelo Endelli/Getty Images Sport/Getty Images, 14–15; David Butler II/USA Today Sports/AP Images, 17, 22–23; Elsa/Getty Images Sport/Getty Images, 18–19; Charles Rex Arbogast/AP Images, 20–21; Eric Gay/AP Images, 24–25; Carmen Mandato/Getty Images Sport/Getty Images, 26–27; Jessica Hill/AP Images, 28–29, 30–31, 40–41, 44–45, 50–51, 58–59; Andy Lyons/Getty Images Sport/Getty Images, 32–33, 34–35; G. Fiume/Getty Images Sport/Getty Images, 36–37; Erica Denhoff/Icon Sportswire/AP Images, 38–39; John Rivera/Icon Sportswire/AP Images, 42–43; Gregory Shamus/Getty Images Sport/Getty Images, 46–47; Lance King/Getty Images Sport/Getty Images, 49; Joe Buglewicz/Getty Images Sport/Getty Images, 52–53; Steph Chambers/Getty Images Sport/Getty Images, 54–55; Don Juan Moore/Getty Images Sport/Getty Images, 56–57

Library of Congress Control Number: 2024951998

ISBN
979-8-89250-722-6 (hardcover)
979-8-89250-774-5 (paperback)
979-8-89250-756-1 (ebook pdf)
979-8-89250-740-0 (hosted ebook)

Printed in the United States of America
Mankato, MN
082025

NOTE TO PARENTS AND EDUCATORS

Apex books are designed to build literacy skills in striving readers. Exciting, high-interest content attracts and holds readers' attention. The text is carefully leveled to allow students to achieve success quickly.

TABLE OF CONTENTS

CHAPTER 1
OVERTIME HERO 4

CHAPTER 2
MINNESOTA MADE 8

IN THE SPOTLIGHT
HOT START 16

CHAPTER 3
THE NEWEST HUSKY 18

CHAPTER 4
INJURY ISSUES 28

CHAPTER 5
COLLEGE STAR 38

IN THE SPOTLIGHT
GREAT GAME 48

CHAPTER 6
UNFINISHED BUSINESS 50

TIMELINE • 58
COMPREHENSION QUESTIONS • 60
GLOSSARY • 62
TO LEARN MORE • 63
ABOUT THE AUTHOR • 63
INDEX • 64

CHAPTER 1

OVERTIME HERO

UConn and NC State were tied 77–77 in double overtime. The teams were playing for a spot in the Final Four. Paige Bueckers caught a pass at the top of the key. She rose up for a three-point shot. It hit nothing but net.

UConn played NC State in the NCAA tournament on March 28, 2022.

Paige Bueckers led UConn in scoring against NC State.

NC State scored to make it 80–79. Then, Bueckers dribbled toward the free-throw line. She hit another shot over three leaping defenders.

Bueckers finished the game with 27 points. She scored 15 of them in overtime. The Huskies won 91–87. They were going back to the Final Four!

HEADING HOME
Beating NC State was special for Bueckers. That year, the Final Four was played in Minneapolis, Minnesota. Bueckers had grown up just a few miles away.

CHAPTER 2

MINNESOTA MADE

Paige Bueckers was born on October 20, 2001, in Edina, Minnesota. She started playing basketball when she was five years old. Paige quickly improved. She often played with older kids.

Edina is a suburb of Minneapolis, Minnesota (pictured).

In sixth grade, Paige did a workout with WNBA coach Cheryl Reeve. Reeve was impressed with Paige's skills.

By seventh grade, Paige starred on Hopkins High School's junior varsity team. The next year, she joined the varsity team. Paige came off the bench in her first game. She drained a three-pointer. Then she made another. Paige made seven three-pointers in a row. The young star was on her way to greatness.

ATTRACTING ATTENTION

Colleges noticed Paige early. She had three scholarship offers before she started high school. One was from the University of Minnesota. Illinois and Iowa State also offered Paige a spot on their teams.

As a freshman, Paige became Hopkins's star player. She led the team to the state championship game that year. However, Hopkins lost. Hopkins lost the state final again the next year. Then came Paige's junior year. She led her team to an undefeated season. Paige was sick on the day of the championship. But she still had 13 points and 7 rebounds. Hopkins won the game 74–45.

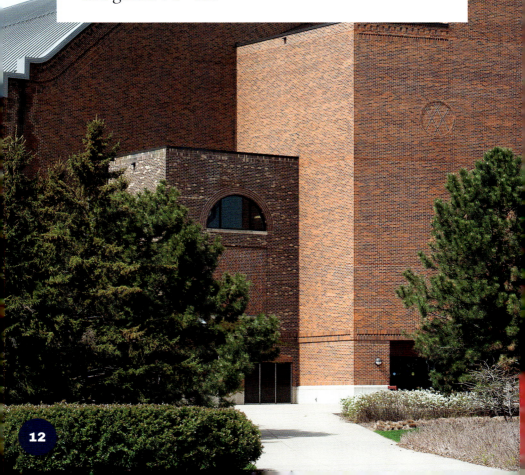

PLAYER OF THE YEAR

Every season, Gatorade names a Player of the Year for each state. Paige won the award three times. She got an even bigger honor after her senior season. She was named the national Gatorade Female Player of the Year.

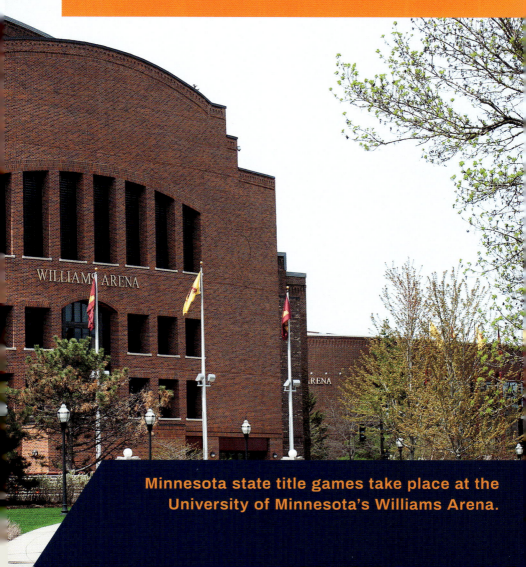

Minnesota state title games take place at the University of Minnesota's Williams Arena.

By Paige's senior year, every college wanted her. She was a great scorer and passer. She could rebound and defend, too. Paige decided to play for the UConn Huskies. But she wanted to win another state title before college. She led Hopkins to another undefeated season. However, the COVID-19 pandemic struck that spring. The state title game was canceled.

TOP RECRUIT

Paige was a five-star recruit. She was the top-ranked player in her grade. That was a big honor. Many other great players graduated from high school that year. They included Caitlin Clark and Angel Reese.

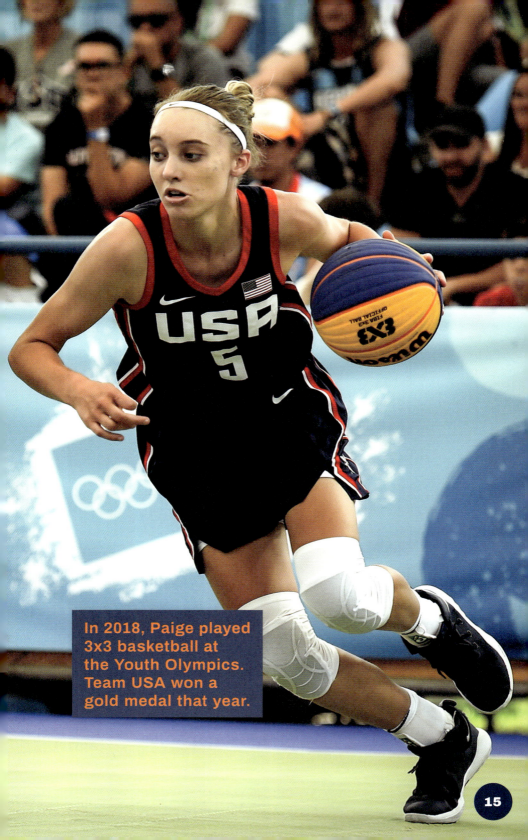

In 2018, Paige played 3x3 basketball at the Youth Olympics. Team USA won a gold medal that year.

IN THE SPOTLIGHT

HOT START

Paige Bueckers made the jump to college look easy. She dominated in her first game at UConn. She drained many shots against the tough college defenders. She made driving layups in the paint. But she was also a threat from long range. Defenders had trouble keeping up. Bueckers led UConn with 17 points. She also had nine rebounds, five assists, and five steals. The first-year star helped the Huskies open the season with a 79–23 blowout.

> **BUECKERS PLAYED IN HER FIRST COLLEGE GAME ON DECEMBER 12, 2020.**

CHAPTER 3

THE NEWEST HUSKY

Many legendary basketball stars have played for UConn. Diana Taurasi was one of them. Growing up, Bueckers idolized Taurasi. Now, Bueckers was determined to make her own mark at UConn.

Diana Taurasi (right) won three straight national championships at UConn from 2002 to 2004.

The 2020–21 Huskies were a young team. Most players were freshmen. Bueckers was ready, though. Right away, she became a strong leader. She played almost every minute of every game.

Huskies coach Geno Auriemma loved Bueckers's maturity. She was a patient player. And she made good decisions. She knew how to wait for the right play to open up on the court.

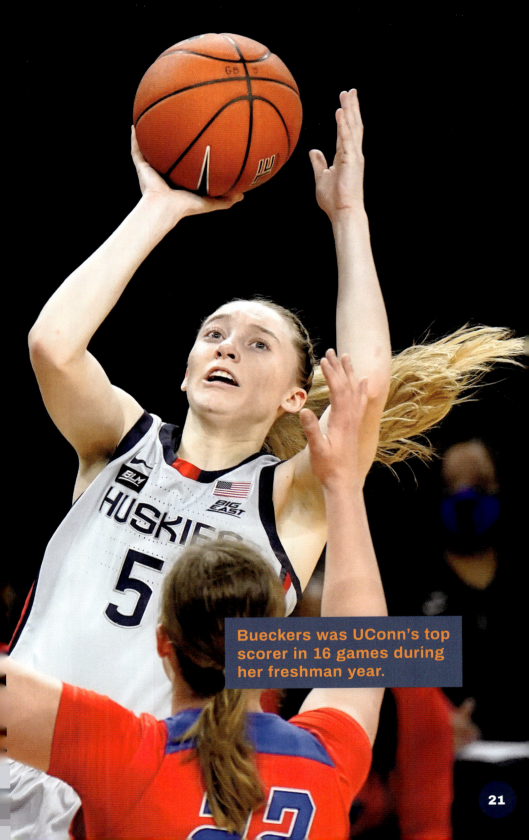
Bueckers was UConn's top scorer in 16 games during her freshman year.

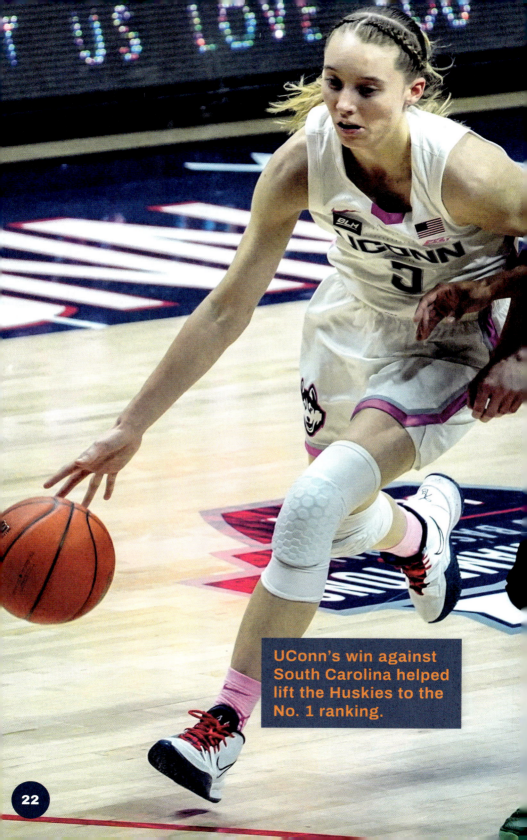

UConn's win against South Carolina helped lift the Huskies to the No. 1 ranking.

In February 2021, the Huskies hosted No. 1 South Carolina. The game went to overtime. Bueckers led UConn with 31 points. She even scored her team's final 13 points. Bueckers also played great defense. She had six steals. UConn won 63–59.

SERIOUS SCORING

Bueckers's 31-point game against South Carolina made history. Two games earlier, she had scored 32 against St. John's. Then, she'd put up 30 against Marquette. She was the first Husky with three straight 30-point games.

UConn finished the regular season 21–1. The Huskies cruised through the first few rounds of the NCAA tournament. Then, UConn faced Baylor in the Elite Eight. Bueckers stepped up again. She scored 28 points. UConn won 69–67. The Huskies went on to the Final Four. But they lost a close game to Arizona.

AWARD WINNER

After her freshman season, Bueckers won the Nancy Lieberman Award. That award goes to the top point guard in the nation. Bueckers was the first freshman to win it.

Bueckers played all 40 minutes of the Baylor game.

Bueckers averaged 20 points per game during the 2020–21 season.

In her first college season, Bueckers led the Huskies in points, assists, and steals. She even set a school record for assists by a freshman. Bueckers also won the Naismith Trophy after her freshman season. It is given to the best player in the country. Bueckers was the first woman to win it as a freshman.

SPEAKING OUT

Bueckers was named the Best College Athlete in women's sports at the 2021 ESPYs. She used her speech to highlight her Black teammates. Bueckers said talented Black players didn't get enough positive attention.

CHAPTER 4

INJURY ISSUES

Guard Azzi Fudd was a top player in the high school class of 2021. Bueckers and Fudd were close friends. They had played together on national youth teams. Bueckers helped convince Fudd to attend UConn.

Bueckers and Azzi Fudd had good chemistry. Bueckers's passes often found Fudd.

Bueckers and Fudd hoped to lead the Huskies to a championship. But Bueckers hurt her left knee in December 2021. She missed half of the season. She didn't get back to the court until February 2022. After that, Bueckers struggled to score. However, the Huskies still reached the NCAA tournament.

LOTS OF FOLLOWERS

Along with many other players, Bueckers helped make women's basketball more popular than ever. She was very active on social media. By 2025, she had more than two million followers on Instagram.

UConn went 22–5 in the 2021–22 regular season. That helped the Huskies earn a No. 2 seed in the NCAA tournament.

Bueckers got back on track in the NCAA tournament. She had another spectacular showing in the Elite Eight. Her 27-point game helped the Huskies take down top-seeded NC State.

In the Final Four, the Huskies faced Stanford. That team was the defending champion. Bueckers was still in pain from her knee injury. But she came through with a big game. She led the Huskies with 14 points. UConn won 63–58.

Bueckers recorded five assists and two steals against Stanford.

Some wondered whether Bueckers would be able to play in the championship game. But she wasn't going to miss the game in her home state of Minnesota. She rested for only one minute of the game. Bueckers led the Huskies with 14 points. It wasn't enough, though. UConn lost to South Carolina 64–49.

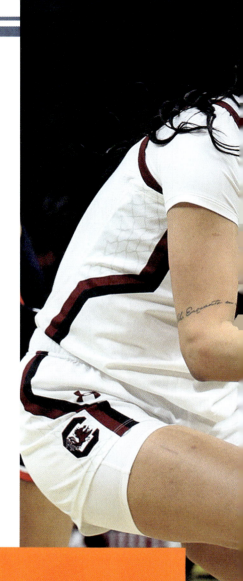

NEW RULES

In 2021, college rules changed. Players were allowed to sign endorsement deals. Many companies wanted to work with Bueckers. She was the first college player to sign with Gatorade. Bueckers also got deals with Nike, Crocs, Nerf, and many other top brands.

Bueckers pulled in six rebounds in the NCAA championship game.

In August 2022, Bueckers was playing pickup basketball. During a game, she hurt her left knee again. The injury caused her to miss the entire 2022–23 season. Without Bueckers, the Huskies struggled. They lost in the Sweet 16.

TALENTED FRIENDS

Paige Bueckers became friends with future Orlando Magic guard Jalen Suggs when they were both in grade school. They were born just a few months apart. They often practiced together. Bueckers and Suggs continued to support each other in college and the pros.

During the 2022–23 season, Bueckers cheered on the Huskies from the bench.

CHAPTER 5

COLLEGE STAR

Some people wondered whether Bueckers would return to UConn after her injury. Many felt that she was ready for the WNBA. But Bueckers decided to return to college for the 2023–24 season.

Bueckers trained hard to recover from her knee injury.

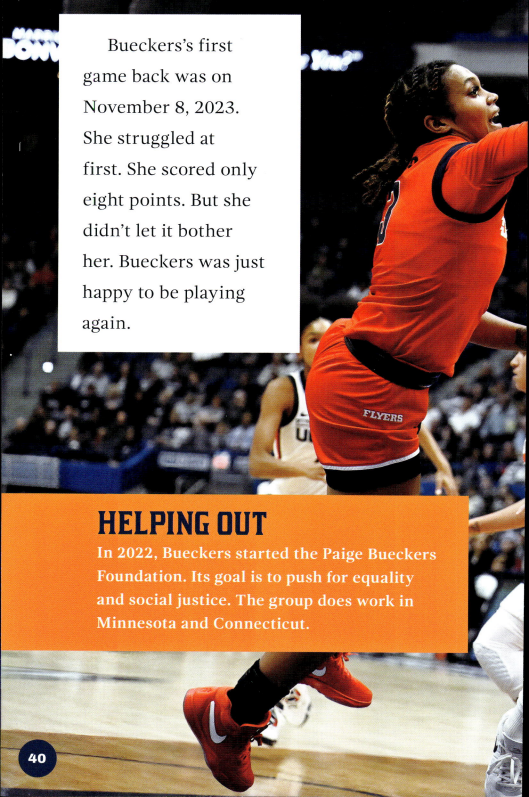

Bueckers's first game back was on November 8, 2023. She struggled at first. She scored only eight points. But she didn't let it bother her. Bueckers was just happy to be playing again.

HELPING OUT

In 2022, Bueckers started the Paige Bueckers Foundation. Its goal is to push for equality and social justice. The group does work in Minnesota and Connecticut.

Bueckers had seven rebounds and four assists in her 2023 return.

Bueckers averaged 21.9 points per game during the 2023–24 season.

More bad luck struck UConn. An injury took out Azzi Fudd. Bueckers had to lead the Huskies alone. She quickly got back to her scoring ways. On December 10, she recorded 26 points against North Carolina. That put her over 1,000 career points. She had reached the mark in just 55 games. That tied a UConn record set by Maya Moore.

PAIGE BUCKETS

Because of her scoring skills, Bueckers became known as "Paige Buckets." She trademarked the nickname in 2021. That way, Bueckers could earn money on items carrying the phrase.

Bueckers was named the Big East Player of the Year for the 2023–24 season. But she saved her best games for the NCAA tournament. In the Huskies' first game, Bueckers scored 28 points. She also added 11 rebounds and 7 assists.

In the next round, Bueckers had 32 points and 10 rebounds. UConn won 72–64. Then, Bueckers led the Huskies to two more wins. Once again, UConn reached the Final Four.

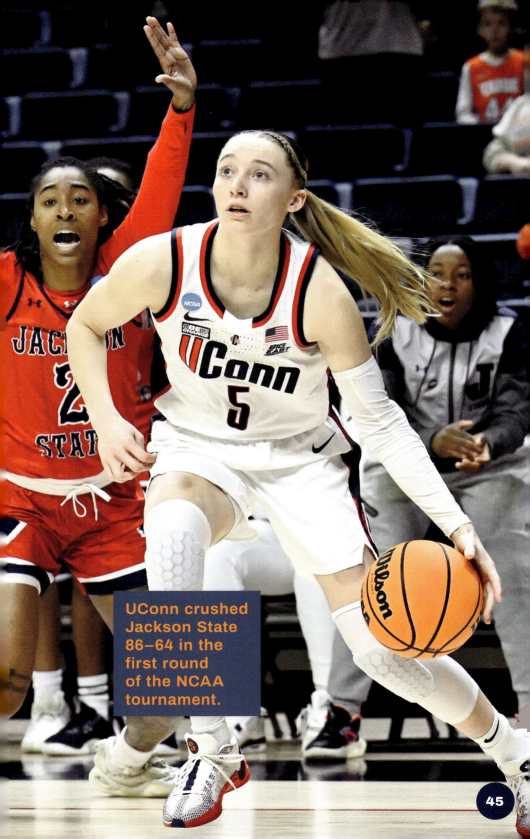

UConn crushed Jackson State 86–64 in the first round of the NCAA tournament.

UConn took on Iowa in the Final Four. It was a showdown between Bueckers and Iowa star Caitlin Clark. Bueckers's smooth shots and crafty passes gave UConn an early lead. But Iowa clawed its way back in the second half. With a few seconds left in the game, Iowa led 70–69. Then, Bueckers received a pass. She was about to shoot. But the whistle blew. The Huskies had been called for a controversial foul. They didn't get the ball back. Iowa won 71–69.

Bueckers scored 17 points in UConn's disappointing loss to Iowa.

IN THE SPOTLIGHT

GREAT GAME

UConn faced USC in the 2024 Elite Eight. Bueckers stepped up for one of the best games of her career. She drained long threes. She dribbled between defenders and weaved her way to the basket. With 4:14 left, UConn led 65–64. Then Bueckers scored 7 of the next 11 points. Bueckers finished the game with a total of 28 points. She also brought in 10 rebounds. UConn pulled away to win 80–73.

BUECKERS SHOT 50 PERCENT FROM THREE-POINT RANGE IN THE ELITE EIGHT.

CHAPTER 6

UNFINISHED BUSINESS

Despite injury struggles, Bueckers had already lifted the Huskies to several deep tournament runs. But she was still hungry for a championship. In 2024–25, she had one more chance to win a title.

UConn blew out Boston University 86–32 in the first game of the 2024–25 season.

Bueckers continued to make smart plays all over the court. She was a selfless passer, a crafty dribbler, and a physical defender. The experienced guard also played with more confidence than ever before. With Bueckers leading the way, UConn was one of the top teams in the nation. The Huskies lost just three games in the regular season.

FINDING FOCUS

Bueckers sometimes felt nervous during games. So, she started seeing a sports psychologist. That helped her stay calm and focused. Even when a game didn't start well, Bueckers stayed positive and bounced back.

In 2024–25, Bueckers led UConn in points and assists.

UConn locked down a No. 2 seed in the 2025 NCAA tournament. Bueckers scored 11 in the first round. She added 34 in the second round.

The veteran star's best performance came in the Sweet 16. Bueckers was deadly from long range. She dropped a career-high 40 points against the No. 3 seed Oklahoma Sooners.

SIGNATURE SHOE

Bueckers released a shoe called the G.T. Hustle 3 in December 2024. She worked with Nike to create it. Bueckers was the first college player to have her own signature shoe.

Bueckers went six for eight from beyond the arc in the 2025 Sweet 16.

Wins in the Elite Eight and Final Four sent UConn to the title game. It was a championship rematch against South Carolina. This time, the Huskies took down the Gamecocks 82–59. Bueckers was a champion at last!

A few days later, the Dallas Wings selected Bueckers with the first pick in the WNBA Draft. She also signed a three-year deal with a professional 3x3 league called Unrivaled. Fans were excited to watch Bueckers in the pros.

Bueckers finished the 2025 title game with 17 points, 6 rebounds, and 3 assists.

TIMELINE

2001 — Paige Bueckers is born in Edina, Minnesota, on October 20.

2015 — As an eighth grader, Paige plays in her first varsity game at Hopkins High School.

2019 — Hopkins High School wins a state championship.

2020 — Bueckers scores 17 points in her first college game.

2021 — Bueckers leads UConn to the Final Four and wins several awards.

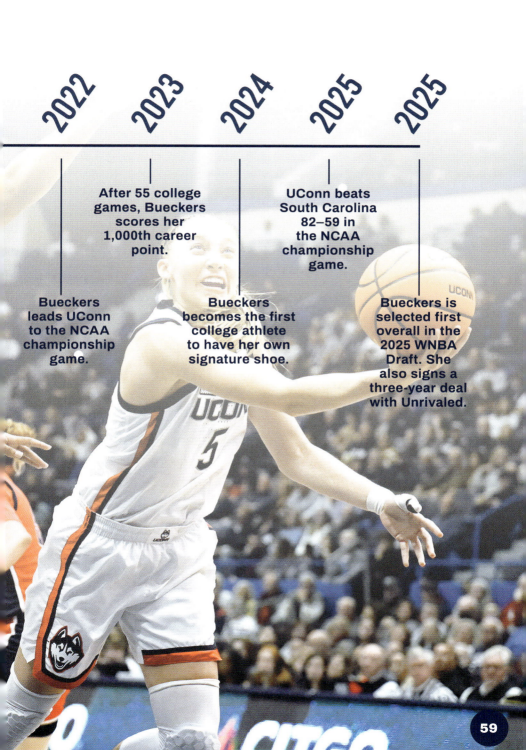

2022 — Bueckers leads UConn to the NCAA championship game.

2023 — After 55 college games, Bueckers scores her 1,000th career point.

2024 — Bueckers becomes the first college athlete to have her own signature shoe.

2025 — UConn beats South Carolina 82–59 in the NCAA championship game.

2025 — Bueckers is selected first overall in the 2025 WNBA Draft. She also signs a three-year deal with Unrivaled.

COMPREHENSION QUESTIONS

Write your answers on a separate piece of paper.

1. Write a short paragraph that explains the main ideas of Chapter 3.

2. What skills do you think helped Paige Bueckers succeed right away in college?

3. In 2022, which school did UConn play in the NCAA championship game?
    - A. USC
    - B. Iowa
    - C. South Carolina

4. How many times did Paige Bueckers play in the Final Four?
    - A. two
    - B. three
    - C. four

5. What does **dominated** mean in this book?

   *Paige Bueckers made the jump to college look easy. She **dominated** in her first game at UConn. She drained many shots against the tough college defenders.*

   A. played better than others
   B. had many difficulties
   C. played worse than expected

6. What does **weaved** mean in this book?

   *She dribbled between defenders and **weaved** her way to the basket.*

   A. ran into people
   B. turned and moved quickly
   C. stopped moving

Answer key on page 64.

GLOSSARY

controversial
Likely to be argued about.

endorsement
When an athlete is paid to support something.

freshman
A first-year student.

idolized
Admired or respected greatly.

maturity
Acting grown-up or like an adult.

overtime
An additional period of play to decide a game's winner.

pandemic
A time when a disease spreads quickly around the world.

psychologist
Someone who studies the mind and how it works.

recruit
An athlete whom college teams are interested in.

scholarship
Money given to someone to help pay for college.

signature
Having to do with a product that was made with help from a top athlete.

varsity
The top team representing a high school or college in a sport or competition.

TO LEARN MORE

BOOKS

Anderson, Josh. *University of Connecticut*. The Child's World, 2024.

Flynn, Brendan. *Girls' Basketball*. Abdo Publishing, 2022.

Sabelko, Rebecca. *Diana Taurasi*. Bellwether Media, 2023.

ONLINE RESOURCES

Visit **www.apexeditions.com** to find links and resources related to this title.

ABOUT THE AUTHOR

Charlie Beattie is a writer and former sportscaster. Originally from Saint Paul, Minnesota, he now lives in Charleston, South Carolina, with his wife and son.

INDEX

Arizona, 24
Auriemma, Geno, 20

Baylor, 24

Clark, Caitlin, 14, 46

Edina, Minnesota, 9
Elite Eight, 24, 32, 48, 56

Final Four, 4, 7, 24, 32, 44, 46, 56
Fudd, Azzi, 28, 30, 43

Hopkins High School, 11–12, 14

Illinois, 11
Iowa, 46
Iowa State, 11

Marquette, 23
Minnesota, University of, 11
Moore, Maya, 43

Naismith Trophy, 27
Nancy Lieberman Award, 24
NCAA tournament, 24, 30, 32, 44, 50, 54
NC State, 4, 7, 32
Nike, 34, 54
North Carolina, 43

Oklahoma, 54

Reese, Angel, 14

South Carolina, 23, 34, 56
Stanford, 32
St. John's, 23
Suggs, Jalen, 36
Sweet 16, 36, 54

Taurasi, Diana, 18

USC, 48

ANSWER KEY:
1. Answers will vary; 2. Answers will vary; 3. C; 4. C; 5. A; 6.